GRAPHIC AMERICA

RADICAL REPUBLICANS

JOHN PERRITANO

Crabtree Publishing Company
www.crabtreebooks.com

Crabtree Publishing Company

www.crabtreebooks.com

Author:
John Perritano
Coordinating editor:
Chester Fisher
Editors:
Scholastic Ventures Inc.
Molly Aloian
Copy editor:
Scholastic Ventures Inc.
Proofreaders:
Adrianna Morganelli
Crystal Sikkens
Project editor:
Robert Walker
Production coordinator:
Katherine Kantor

Prepress technicians:
Ken Wright
Katherine Kantor
Logo design:
Samantha Crabtree
Project manager:
Santosh Vasudevan (Q2AMedia)
Art direction:
Rahul Dhiman (Q2AMedia)
Design:
Tarang Saggar (Q2AMedia)
Photographs:
Alamy: North Wind Picture Archives: p. 19
Illustrations:
Q2AMedia

Library and Archives Canada Cataloguing in Publication

Perritano, John
Radical Republicans / John Perritano.

(Graphic America)
Includes index.
ISBN 978-0-7787-4187-9 (bound).--ISBN 978-0-7787-4214-2 (pbk.)

1. Reconstruction (U.S. history, 1865-1877)--Comic books, strips, etc.--Juvenile literature. 2. United States--Politics and government--1865-1877--Comic books, strips, etc.--Juvenile literature. 3. Republican Party (U.S. : 1854-)--Comic books, strips, etc.--Juvenile literature. 4. Radicalism--United States--History--19th century--Comic books, strips, etc.--Juvenile literature. I. Title. II. Series.

E668.P47 2008 j973.8 C2008-906284-1

Library of Congress Cataloging-in-Publication Data

Perritano, John.
Radical Republicans / John Perritano.
p. cm. -- (Graphic America)
Includes index.
ISBN-13: 978-0-7787-4214-2 (pbk. : : alk. paper)
ISBN-10: 0-7787-4214-8 (pbk. : : alk. paper)
ISBN-13: 978-0-7787-4187-9 (reinforced library binding : alk. paper)
ISBN-10: 0-7787-4187-7 (reinforced library binding : alk. paper)
1. Reconstruction (U.S. history, 1865-1877)--Comic books, strips, etc.--Juvenile literature. 2. United States--Politics and government--1865-1877--Comic books, strips, etc.--Juvenile literature. 3. Republican Party (U.S. : 1854-)--Comic books, strips, etc.--Juvenile literature. 4. Radicalism--United States--History--19th century--Comic books, strips, etc.--Juvenile literature. 5. Graphic novels. I. Title. II. Series.

E668.P45 2009
973.8--dc22

2008041853

Crabtree Publishing Company

www.crabtreebooks.com 1-800-387-7650

Published in Canada
Crabtree Publishing
616 Welland Ave.
St. Catharines, ON
L2M 5V6

Published in the United States
Crabtree Publishing
PMB16A
350 Fifth Ave., Suite 3308
New York, NY 10118

Published in the United Kingdom
Crabtree Publishing
White Cross Mills
High Town, Lancaster
LA1 4XS

Published in Australia
Crabtree Publishing
386 Mt. Alexander Rd.
Ascot Vale (Melbourne)
VIC 3032

CONTENTS

"MALICE TOWARD NONE"

AS 1865 BEGAN, THE END OF THE CIVIL WAR WAS NEAR. HUNDREDS OF THOUSANDS OF AMERICANS DIED IN DOZENS OF BATTLES, SUCH AS BULL RUN, GETTYSBURG, AND SHILOH. THE SOUTH, WHICH **SECEDED** FROM THE UNITED STATES FOUR YEARS BEFORE, WAS IN RUINS. UNION ARMIES FROM THE NORTH HAD DESTROYED THE GREAT **PLANTATIONS**. VIOLENCE LEFT CITIES AND TOWNS IN SHAMBLES. THE WAR BROUGHT FREEDOM TO THE SLAVES.
IT SURE HAS BEEN A LONG WAR.
I SIGNED UP AFTER BULL RUN AND FOUGHT STRAIGHT THROUGH.

WITH MALICE TOWARD NONE, WITH CHARITY FOR ALL, WITH FIRMNESS IN THE RIGHT...LET US STRIVE ON TO FINISH THE WORK WE ARE IN, TO BIND UP THE NATION'S WOUNDS.*
WITH VICTORY NEAR, PRESIDENT ABRAHAM LINCOLN MADE A PLAN TO BRING THE SOUTH BACK INTO THE UNION. HE CALLED THE PLAN RECONSTRUCTION. LINCOLN WANTED TO WELCOME THE REBELLIOUS SOUTH WITH OPEN ARMS. HE SPOKE OF HIS PLAN DURING HIS SECOND ***INAUGURATION.***

THIS WILL HAVE THE BEST POSSIBLE EFFECT UPON THE MEN.
I SHALL INSTRUCT THE OFFICERS...TO LET ALL THE MEN WHO CLAIM TO OWN A HORSE OR MULE TAKE THE ANIMALS HOME WITH THEM TO THEIR LITTLE FARMS.*
ON APRIL 9, CONFEDERATE GENERAL ROBERT E. LEE SURRENDERED HIS ARMY TO UNION GENERAL ULYSSES S. GRANT. THE REST OF THE CONFEDERATE ARMY WOULD SOON LAY DOWN THEIR GUNS. GRANT AND LEE TOOK THE FIRST STEP IN THE PROCESS OF REUNITING THE COUNTRY. GRANT WAS VERY GENEROUS TO THE DEFEATED REBEL ARMY. HE LET THEM TAKE THEIR ANIMALS HOME TO REBUILD THEIR FARMS.

**ACTUAL QUOTE*

I HAVE ALWAYS THOUGHT "DIXIE" WAS ONE OF THE BEST TUNES I HAVE EVER HEARD.※
LINCOLN WAS HAPPY WHEN HE HEARD THE NEWS OF LEE'S SURRENDER. HE WANTED TO HEAR ONE OF HIS FAVORITE SONGS, "DIXIE," THE **ANTHEM** OF THE CONFEDERACY.

MANY REPUBLICANS IN CONGRESS WANTED TO PUNISH THE SOUTH FOR STARTING THE WAR. THEY DID NOT WANT SLAVE OWNERS TO RETURN TO POWER. THE REPUBLICANS WANTED EQUAL RIGHTS FOR FREED SLAVES. THESE LAWMAKERS, SUCH AS SENATOR THADDEUS STEVENS, WERE KNOWN AS RADICAL REPUBLICANS.
IF WE DO NOT FURNISH FREED SLAVES WITH HOMESTEADS, AND IF WE LEAVE THEM TO THE LEGISLATION OF THEIR LATE MASTERS, WE HAD BETTER HAVE LEFT THEM IN BONDAGE.※

※ACTUAL QUOTE

RADICAL REPUBLICANS BELIEVED CONGRESS, NOT THE PRESIDENT, SHOULD BE IN CHARGE OF RECONSTRUCTION. ON APRIL 15, 1865, AN **ASSASSIN** SHOT AND KILLED ABRAHAM LINCOLN. LINCOLN'S "MALICE TOWARD NONE" PLAN ENDED WITH HIS DEATH.

PRESIDENTIAL RECONSTRUCTION BEGINS

THE SOUTH IS NOT A SEPARATE CONQUERED NATION, AND WE WILL TREAT THEM AS SUCH.
MR. PRESIDENT, WHAT IS YOUR VIEW ON RECONSTRUCTION?
ANDREW JOHNSON, A FORMER SLAVE OWNER, BECAME THE 17TH PRESIDENT OF THE UNITED STATES. JOHNSON BELIEVED THAT "WHITE MEN ALONE MUST MANAGE THE SOUTH."

JOHNSON PARDONED THOUSANDS OF CONFEDERATES. HE ALLOWED VOTERS TO CHOOSE FORMER CONFEDERATE LEADERS TO STATE LEGISLATURES.
I PROMISE TO RETURN THE SOUTH TO ITS GLORY DAYS, WHEN THE WHITE MAN WAS FREE AND THE BLACK MAN WAS HIS SLAVE.

JUDGE, JUDGE, GIVE ME MY BOY BACK.
MAMA, I DON'T WANT TO GO. MAMA, WHY ARE THEY TAKIN' ME AWAY?
THESE LAWMAKERS SOON PASSED LAWS CALLED "BLACK CODES." THESE CODES WERE ANOTHER FORM OF SLAVERY. SOME LAWS ALLOWED COURTS TO TAKE AFRICAN AMERICAN CHILDREN AWAY FROM THEIR PARENTS AND MAKE THEM WORK FOR WHITE EMPLOYERS.

NO JOB, NO FOOD. WE'RE NO BETTER OFF THAN WE WERE AS SLAVES.
OTHER LAWS MADE IT HARD FOR FREED SLAVES TO OWN PROPERTY OR RENT HOUSES. THE GOVERNMENT **ABOLISHED** SLAVERY, BUT AFRICAN AMERICANS WERE FAR FROM FREE.

RADICAL REPUBLICANS TAKE CONTROL

THE WHOLE FABRIC OF SOUTHERN SOCIETY MUST BE CHANGED.※
*THE RADICAL REPUBLICANS DID NOT LIKE THE WAY PRESIDENT JOHNSON WAS HANDLING RECONSTRUCTION. IN 1866, THEY TOOK CONTROL OF CONGRESS. CONGRESS COULD NOW **OVERRIDE** ANY PRESIDENTIAL **VETOES**. THE RADICALS PASSED THEIR OWN RECONSTRUCTION LAWS.*

※ACTUAL QUOTE

QUICKLY, THE RADICALS PASSED THE CIVIL RIGHTS ACT OF 1866, GIVING AFRICAN AMERICANS MORE CIVIL RIGHTS. BUT THEY COULD STILL NOT VOTE OR SIT ON A JURY.
FINALLY, WE HAVE RIGHTS. WE NEVER HAD RIGHTS BEFORE.
BLACKS HAVE RIGHTS

RACE RIOTS

IN MAY 1866, A RIOT BROKE OUT BETWEEN AFRICAN AMERICANS AND WHITES IN MEMPHIS, TENNESSEE. THE RIOT STARTED WHEN WHITES BELIEVED A GROUP OF AFRICAN AMERICAN SOLDIERS HAD KILLED SEVERAL POLICE OFFICERS. A GROUP OF ANGRY WHITE MEN ATTACKED THE HOMES OF NEWLY FREED SLAVES.

ABOUT FORTY-SIX AFRICAN AMERICANS AND TWO WHITES DIED IN THE FIGHTING.

IN JULY, FORMER CONFEDERATE SOLDIERS AND POLICE OFFICERS BEAT UP A GROUP OF RADICAL REPUBLICANS AND AFRICAN AMERICANS MEETING IN NEW ORLEANS. THIRTY-FOUR AFRICAN AMERICANS AND THREE RADICAL REPUBLICANS DIED.

CONGRESSIONAL RECONSTRUCTION

THE VIOLENCE PROVED TO CONGRESS THAT THEY NEEDED TO TREAT THE SOUTH DIFFERENTLY THAN THE REST OF THE COUNTRY. CONGRESS DECLARED ***MARTIAL LAW*** *PUTTING THE SOUTH UNDER THE CONTROL OF ARMY SOLDIERS.*

THOSE YANKEES ARE BACK, JUST LIKE DURING THE WAR.
PA SAYS THEY'RE NOT WELCOME 'ROUND HERE.

CONGRESS ALSO DECIDED THAT IF SOUTHERN STATES WANTED BACK INTO THE UNION, EACH STATE HAD TO **RATIFY** THE FOURTEENTH AMENDMENT TO THE U.S. CONSTITUTION. THE AMENDMENT GRANTED CITIZENSHIP TO FREED SLAVES.

CONGRESS IMPEACHES THE PRESIDENT

PRESIDENT JOHNSON DID NOT AGREE WITH THE LAWS CONGRESS HAD PASSED. HE VETOED MANY OF THEM. CONGRESS OVERRODE JOHNSON'S VETOES.
...IT IS THE OBJECT OF THESE LAWS TO CONFER UPON NEGROES THE PRIVILEGE OF VOTING...IT IS NOT PROPOSED MERELY THAT THEY SHALL GOVERN THEMSELVES, BUT THAT THEY SHALL RULE THE WHITE RACE.*

*ACTUAL QUOTE

JOHNSON COULD NOT STOP CONGRESS FROM PASSING LAWS. HE COULD WEAKEN THEM, HOWEVER. JOHNSON FIRED PEOPLE WHO WERE TRYING TO ENFORCE THE LAW. ONE OF THOSE OFFICIALS WAS SECRETARY OF WAR EDWIN STANTON.
SECRETARY STANTON, I'M AFRAID WE DO NOT AGREE ON MANY ISSUES. I MUST ASK YOU TO LEAVE.
YOU ARE THE PRESIDENT OF A FREE COUNTRY, SIR, NOT A TYRANT!

ANDREW JOHNSON, PRESIDENT OF THE UNITED STATES...DID ATTEMPT TO BRING INTO DISGRACE THE CONGRESS OF THE UNITED STATES.*
CONGRESS WAS ANGRY WITH JOHNSON. THE HOUSE OF REPRESENTATIVES VOTED TO **IMPEACH**, OR REMOVE, THE PRESIDENT FROM OFFICE.

*ACTUAL QUOTE

TRIAL IN THE SENATE

IT WAS NOW UP TO THE SENATE TO DETERMINE IF JOHNSON WAS RIGHT OR WRONG IN HIS ACTIONS. SENATOR CHARLES SUMNER, THE LEADER OF THE RADICAL REPUBLICANS, ARGUED AGAINST JOHNSON.
SLAVERY HAS BEEN OUR WORST ENEMY...AND NOW IT REARS ITS CREST ANEW, WITH ANDREW JOHNSON AS ITS REPRESENTATIVE.*

*ACTUAL QUOTE

SOME DID NOT WANT TO REMOVE JOHNSON JUST BECAUSE HE DID NOT AGREE WITH CONGRESS. BY ONE VOTE, THE SENATE FOUND JOHNSON NOT GUILTY.

THE RIGHT TO VOTE

I FEEL AS THOUGH I'M DREAMIN'.
WE WERE ONCE CONSIDERED PROPERTY, NOW WE ARE TRULY CITIZENS.

IN FEBRUARY 1869, CONGRESS PASSED A CONSTITUTIONAL AMENDMENT GIVING AFRICAN AMERICANS THE RIGHT TO VOTE. IN 1870, THE FIFTEENTH AMENDMENT WAS ADDED TO THE U.S. CONSTITUTION.

PEOPLE VOTED HUNDREDS OF AFRICAN AMERICANS INTO PUBLIC OFFICE. THIS ANGERED MANY SOUTHERNERS. IN GEORGIA, DEMOCRATS IN THE LEGISLATURE TRIED TO THROW OUT NEWLY CHOSEN AFRICAN AMERICAN MEMBERS.
I'LL DO ANYTHING IN MY POWER TO KEEP THESE "SLAVES" FROM HOLDING OFFICE.
THIS IS AN OUTRAGE!

NEWLY ELECTED AFRICAN AMERICANS, INCLUDING HENRY MCNEAL TURNER, DEFENDED THEIR RIGHTS TO TAKE OFFICE.
I HOLD THAT I AM A MEMBER OF THIS BODY...WE ASK YOU NOW FOR OUR RIGHTS.*

*ACTUAL QUOTE

THE FREEDMEN'S BUREAU

THESE CHILDREN HAVE NEVER BEEN IN A SCHOOLHOUSE BEFORE. DO YOU THINK I CAN HELP THEM?
DON'T WORRY MISS STEPHENS. YOU CAME HERE TO HELP OUR PEOPLE, AND YOU WILL.
THE FREEDMEN'S BUREAU WAS IMPORTANT DURING RECONSTRUCTION. THE BUREAU'S JOB WAS TO HELP FREED SLAVES. THE BUREAU SET UP NEW SCHOOLS FOR AFRICAN AMERICANS.

THE FREEDMEN'S BUREAU GAVE FOOD AND MEDICINE TO FORMER SLAVES...

AND PROTECTED THEM...

AND HELPED THEM FIND HOMES.
ROOMS AVAILABLE

CARPETBAGGERS

JUST WHAT WE NEED, MORE CARPETBAGGERS IN TOWN.
THEY'LL STEAL THE COAT RIGHT OFF YOUR BACK, OR A PENNY OUT OF YOUR POCKET.

*SOUTHERNERS **SCORNFULLY** CALLED THE NORTHERNERS "CARPETBAGGERS." THE WORD CAME FROM THE TYPE OF BAG TRAVELERS USED AT THE TIME. THE BAG WAS MADE FROM CARPET. THE SOUTHERNERS THOUGHT CARPETBAGGERS WERE CROOKS.*

MOST OF THE CARPETBAGGERS WORKED FOR THE FREEDMEN'S BUREAU. SOME CARPETBAGGERS, HOWEVER, WERE DISHONEST PEOPLE WORKING IN OTHER PARTS OF THE GOVERNMENT.
HERE'S THE MONEY YOU ASKED FOR, MY GOOD FRIEND. I HOPE WE CAN DO BUSINESS.
I'M CERTAIN THAT WE CAN.

THE END OF RECONSTRUCTION

MANY WHITE SOUTHERNERS WERE AGAINST THE GOVERNMENT'S RECONSTRUCTION PLANS. MANY STATES VOTED RADICAL REPUBLICANS OUT OF OFFICE. THE KU KLUX KLAN USED VIOLENCE TO ATTACK THE FREEDMEN AND THEIR WHITE SUPPORTERS.
WE DON'T TAKE TOO KINDLY TO STRANGERS TELLIN' US WHAT TO DO. LEAVE AND NEVER COME BACK!

WHEN THE LAST SOLDIERS LEFT THE SOUTH IN 1877, RECONSTRUCTION WAS OVER. SOUTHERN POLITICIANS PASSED LAWS THAT TOOK AWAY THE AFRICAN AMERICANS' CIVIL RIGHTS. THE SOUTH WAS **SEGREGATED** ONCE AGAIN. IT WOULD TAKE MANY YEARS BEFORE THEY WOULD REGAIN THEIR CIVIL RIGHTS.

TIMELINE

1865 – IN MARCH, PRESIDENT ABRAHAM LINCOLN OUTLINES HIS PLAN FOR RECONSTRUCTION ASKING THE COUNTRY TO WELCOME BACK THE SOUTH WITH "CHARITY FOR ALL."

1865 – IN APRIL, PRESIDENT ABRAHAM LINCOLN IS ASSASSINATED; ANDREW JOHNSON BECOMES THE 17TH PRESIDENT OF THE UNITED STATES.

1865 – IN MAY, THE U.S. CIVIL WAR ENDS.

1865 – IN DECEMBER, THE THIRTEENTH AMENDMENT, WHICH ABOLISHES SLAVERY, IS ADDED TO THE U.S. CONSTITUTION.

1866 – CONGRESS PASSES THE CIVIL RIGHTS ACT OF 1866 OVER PRESIDENT JOHNSON'S VETO. THE LAW GIVES AFRICAN AMERICANS MORE CIVIL RIGHTS.

1868 – IN FEBRUARY, THE HOUSE OF REPRESENTATIVES VOTES TO IMPEACH PRESIDENT JOHNSON. IN MAY, THE SENATE FINDS JOHNSON NOT GUILTY.

1868 – IN JULY, THE FOURTEENTH AMENDMENT, GIVING CITIZENSHIP TO FREED SLAVES, IS ADDED TO THE CONSTITUTION.

1870 – THE FIFTEENTH AMENDMENT, GIVING AFRICAN AMERICAN MEN THE RIGHT TO VOTE, IS ADDED TO THE CONSTITUTION.

1877 – THE LAST FEDERAL TROOPS LEAVE THE SOUTH.

GLOSSARY

ABOLISHED BROUGHT TO AN END

ANTHEM A SONG OR HYMN OF PRAISE OR GLADNESS

ASSASSIN A MURDERER WHO KILLS A FAMOUS PERSON

CIVIL RIGHTS THE RIGHTS A PERSON HAS BECAUSE HE OR SHE IS A CITIZEN

IMPEACH TO REMOVE FROM OFFICIAL OFFICE; TO BRING CHARGES AGAINST

INAUGURATION A CEREMONY THAT INTRODUCES SOMEONE INTO AN ELECTED OFFICE

LEGISLATURE A GROUP OF PEOPLE HAVING THE POWER TO MAKE LAWS

MARTIAL LAW A LAW BROUGHT ABOUT BY THE MILITARY IN AN EMERGENCY

OVERRIDE TO SET ASIDE; OVERRULE

PARDONED RELEASED FROM THE PENALTIES OF A CRIME

PLANTATION A VERY LARGE FARM

RATIFY TO ACCEPT AS A LAW

SCORNFULLY ANGRILY; DISGUSTEDLY

SECEDED BROKEN AWAY FROM

SEGREGATED SEPARATION OF THE RACES

VETO THE POWER OF A PRESIDENT TO REJECT A BILL PASSED BY THE LEGISLATURE TO PREVENT IT FROM BECOMING LAW

INDEX

WEBFINDER

HTTP://WWW.DIGITALHISTORY.UH.EDU/RECONSTRUCTION/INDEX.HTML

HTTP://WWW.WHITEHOUSE.GOV/HISTORY/PRESIDENTS/AL16.HTML

HTTP://WWW.WHITEHOUSE.GOV/HISTORY/PRESIDENTS/AJ17.HTML

HTTP://MEMORY.LOC.GOV/AMMEM/AAOHTML/EXHIBIT/AOPART5.HTML

HTTP://WWW.ARCHIVES.GOV/RESEARCH/AFRICAN-AMERICANS/FREEDMENS-BUREAU/